FIFTY
POEMS
ABOUT
CHRISTMAS

by

Vito Gentile

Request for permission to make copies of any part of this work should be made to August First Arts, P.O. Box 311, East Quogue, NY 11942, or augustfirstarts@aol.com.

Printed in the United States of America
First Printing 2007, Second Printing 2012

ISBN Number: 978-0-9884967-1-2
Library of Congress Control Number: 2012919750

I dedicate this volume to my sister Mickey, who loved Christmas more than anyone I have ever known; for calling me up on the twenty-fourth of every month (starting with January) to ask if I had begun my Christmas shopping, for all the hand-made ornaments she made over the years that adorn my Christmas tree, for her glorious gift-wrapping that screamed Christmas, for all the holiday books and movies we shared over a lifetime, and for being my greatest friend and the inspiration for so many of my Christmas poems, including those rhyming ones that I fondly think of as Mickey-poems.

I

II

Acknowledgement

Before we begin, I would like to thank those who have inspired me to write all my Christmas poems over these many years; those of you who called to see if the annual poems had been written, those who patiently listened to drafts being read over the phone, and those who came around to check the grammar and spelling.

Most importantly I would like to thank those who created the designs and gave me the confidence to put the poems in the mail. Without their input this dyslexic writer would never have flourished.

From the bottom of my heart I thank you all and will always keep you in my prayers.

Sincerely,
Vito Gentile

Christmas

A great time to remember back when
An even greater time to remember why

Christmas Cards: at first we leave them on the
dining room table stuck in their envelopes, and
wonder why some people have so much time to
send them so early. Later, if one is pretty, we might
stick it in the corner of a mirror or a picture frame –
a little color to get the holiday going.

As their numbers grow, we start standing them up
like little toy soldiers on the mantel, between books
in the bookcase, next to the lamp in the hall. As the
days go by and the army of cards gets too big and
their corners start getting droopy and we've grown
tired of standing them back up, we toss them into
big bowls or into wicker baskets filled with holiday
ribbons. The adventurous hang them from festive
ribbons across a wall, or down a wall, or along a
cornice in the family playroom.

Closer to Christmas, amid our shopping, our cooking, and our holidaying, we take a moment here and there to look into that bowl or onto that string and read the salutations, and subconsciously as we read the handwriting we count the names and ponder "Is everyone well? Has much changed in a year?" We pencil notes to give so-and-so a call once the festivities quiet down, and wonder if they received our card and if they liked it.

Once Christmas has passed, the leftovers have all been eaten and the tree taken down, we finally feel the moment is right to read all those lovely greetings in those Christmas cards we have so admired hanging around our homes.

As you can see from the above statement I have spent a lifetime observing Christmas card habits, along with how we prepare for and spend our Christmas holidays. Since I was a child I have always been fascinated by Christmas. Perhaps it is because I truly love Christmastime more than any other time of the year, and perhaps that is why I've also spent a lifetime writing Christmas poems, which are by far my favorite ones to write.

As you go through my collection, you'll notice that there are no dates shown. The reason for this is that circumstances have everything to do with what I write. I might start a poem in January – sometimes while the decorations are still up – but then as the year progresses and circumstances change, new insights arise and a second or third poem is born. Some of these poems have never been seen, others have found their way onto the front of a Christmas card a few years down the road. So I haven't given dates to avoid confusion for the reader who has saved some of these cards and wants to cross-reference the poems against the originals. Oh, did I mention that I also have a habit of rewriting them? All I can say is, it's a wonderful process!

Enjoy the poems, and Merry Christmas!

That one moment

When for no apparent reason

The memories of your childhood

Of friends

And most of all, loved ones

Condense into a single teardrop

Appearing indiscriminately in the corner

Of one of your eyes

Is known as Christmas

Go out into the streets and smile

For you have license

Be joyous and generous with others

Squander emotions

And replenish your childhood

For today is for celebrating

The birthday of a King

On a tiny little pine needle

Through the distant whistle of a Christmas carol

A church bell rings

Off-key children sing

People pray prayers of dreams

And memories fall from an angel's wing

Through the distant whistle of a Christmas carol

On a tiny little pine needle

It is the longest night of the year
Dark clouds hover over the earth
Stars in formation hang in the sky

A new star –
A bright star spins excitedly through the universe
Angels, many angels, gathering in the heavens
Prepare to sing a glorious new song

Down on Earth –
Families move slowly along winding roads
Looking for shelter from the night air
A young couple and their donkey are among them

In the small town of Bethlehem
The shopkeepers are shutting down for the night
Shepherds and their flocks journey towards their stable

It was the longest night of the year

Glorious, Glorious

Sounds of Christmas

Sing in the ears

Of those who dream

Christmas rides a city bus

Peering out at the shop windows

It sits in the clutter of cathedrals

At the bottom of a bottle

On the sour note of an old song

It shoulders in at a dinner table

Basks in the aroma of rich foods

And silly conversation

It stands on the edge of a kiss

At both ends of a kindness

At the point of a smile

I have a small star

It sits on top of my tree

It lights

Red

And lights go up and down its sides twinkling

And some do not

Candles stand and some are slanted so

Slanted with everything

Covered with horses and angels

And glass things and tinsel

A locomotive runs with lots of cars

On lots of track

It smokes – whistles too!

It circles around and around

Around gifts and toys

Wrapped in colors red and green that don't match

Except for tags

To: From: With Love:

And Merry Christmas

Paper snowflakes taped to windows, sills covered
with rubber dolls waving to curious faces reflected
in the windowpanes.

Indoor/outdoor green and blue lights cascade up
and down, in and out of the pickets of a wrought
iron fence, inviting young school children to pluck
at them.

Circles of lacquered pinecones with gold velveteen
ribbons nailed to front door after front door, beckon
visitors near.

While up on the rooftops 100-watt Santas laugh and
blink, laugh and blink, as a trillion tin angels sing
"Adeste Fideles!"

A

Tree

Is plugged in

A baby giggles

And crawls forward

A mother reaches out

A daddy's eyes well with tears

A new Christmas begins

Christmas

You old perennial spirit

Shower your children with sparkle and chime

Ignite our faces, our hearts with infinite innocence

Consume us with your joyful magic

And your generosity and love

There's always room for faith at Christmastime

For carols, calories and prayer

There's always room for charity at Christmastime

For shopping, cavorting and care

There's always room for love at Christmastime

For memories, strangers and a kiss

There's always room for hope at Christmastime

For daydreams, promises and bliss

A camel and a star stood on the side of a cellophane hill next to a silver blender. An angel, with real angel's hair, sat atop a cardboard stable peering down at the Madonna and the stalking family dog.

The Madonna was frantic. The exhaust fan was blowing straw off the refrigerator. Joseph and a small flock of assorted sheep seemed next. Eager little stubby fingers on scuffed tippy-toes lay in wait to take a surprised statuette off to bed.

Wise men wobbled in their wooden robes. An innkeeper gently tapped against a glass sugar bowl. A small flock tipped and a hand-painted shepherd hit his head on a red canister. Clink! The Infant awoke. "W-AAAAAAAAA!!!"

The family dog barked and skidded across the straw seasoned kitchen floor. The little stubby fingers on scuffed tippy-toes made a leap for the hand-painted shepherd, missed and she was scooted off to bed. The family dog was scooted too.

The camel laughed. The star tried not to, but also laughed. The Madonna sighed. They tried to stop, because they knew they should, but couldn't, and only laughed harder.

The Infant cried louder. The angel with real angel's hair, rolled her eyes towards the florescent heavens, and the Madonna, who held no malice towards the camel and the star nor the exhaust fan for that matter, resigned herself to a long sleepless night.

Joseph just prayed for peace. The hand-painted shepherd, who hit his head on the red canister and barely escaped abduction, apologized and joined in the prayer. The innkeeper, near the sugar bowl, also prayed.

Even the wise men in wooden robes prayed, as did assorted sheep in small flocks, and finally, the camel and the star tried to control themselves and sort of prayed. They all prayed and kept on praying till the hum-da-la-hum of the defrost cycle rocked the Infant back to sleep.

And soon the Infant, in His slumber, was joined by the little stubby fingers senza scuffed tippy-toes, assorted sheep, the family dog, wise men in their wooden robes, and yes, even the camel and the star, who promised to act like adults, were asleep on the side of the cellophane hill, next to the silver blender.

And the world found itself once more at peace, held in the amber glow of a night-light and the hum-da-la-hum of a Merry Christmas.

Turn-on to television

See Christmas

In the specials that once

And always tug at your heart

Turn around a corner

Listen to the carols

That once and still inspire

Turn through a revolving door

Experience the wonders

Of Christmas past

And presents purchased

Turn a knob

Enter the home

Of those who love

Amid the fancy lights

And twinkling wrappings

Turn onto Christmas

Its magic

Its spirit

And its persistence!

A

Train

Circles a tree

In a forest of corporate

Wizards conversing on the subjects

Of profits, plum puddings, and size AA batteries

Oh, yes, the

Wonders of

Christmas!

The echoes of chimes through a cold night
The dreams of small children, like reindeer in flight
The boldness of plaid, in ribbons and wrap
The plushness of tissue that fills in the gap

The legends of angels from tree tops and books
The aromas of recipes, cookies and cooks
The bargains in basements, the sale's items tossed
The parties, the friendships, the addresses lost

The excitement of snowflakes, the traffic that sings
The giggles at photos, and joys that they bring
The Santas on corners, toy trestles and trains
The relatives who visit by subways and planes

The Child in the crèche, the sound of a choir
The lights on a lawn, the logs on a fire
The trees in the windows, the wreaths on the doors
The hugs in a greeting and Clement Clark Moore's

"Happy Christmas to all, and to all a Good Night!"

21

Christmas

A word

A date

A season

A way of life

And an angel

Said to an angel

Who said to an angel

Come, let us line-up along the wire –

The wire that cuts across the moon

Let us put our spirit forward and listen with haste

To the sound of the sheep

The sheep that grazes alone in the field

To the bird soaring high above the earth

The fish splashing atop the coldest of seas

Listen to the wind as it rustles in the hills

To the stone skipping across a darkened path

To a leaf falling, a lamp burning

Straw crunching beneath the foot of man

To a fire crackling as a young mother sighs

Come listen to the cry of a new born Babe

As angels sing songs of peace

Say a prayer for the makers

Of Christmas memories

Be they here

Or gone

Or yet to come

Carolers in woolen sweaters

On hard wooden benches

Practice descants

Evergreen vendors

In canvas mitts hover around makeshift stoves

Mothers in cotton aprons scan grandmas' recipes

Dads in corduroy windbreakers

Negotiate clumps of lights and aluminum ladders

While lines of children in bright snowsuits

Spiral through Santa's workshop

Waiting with anticipation --

Waiting for the elf in the crimson tunic to yell

"Next!"

Floating through the air in mailbags

In cartons in backs of trucks and on speeding trains

Folded between Christmas catalogues

And all those maddening December bills

Greetings arrive from friends, from family

From persons across the hall, from the next desk

"Merry Christmas" they read, "Happy Holidays,"

"A Good New Year"

They stand on tables

Hang from ribbons across and down a wall

Even taped, sometimes, to the back of a front door

We enjoy looking at them

Talking about them and the price of stamps

Each a quiet acknowledgment that all is well

A comforting thought at the sum of the year

Caesar Augustus they say

Decreed a census be taken that first Christmas

He wanted a tally of his world

And in our own way, so do we!

In the touch of a snowflake
The skid of a boot
The bite of the ice

In the wrap of a scarf
The tug of a hat
The grab of a rail

In the press of a bell
The knock on a door
The turn of a knob

In the squeeze of a hug
The shake of a hand
The smack of a kiss

In the lift of a glass
The pull of a ribbon
The warmth of a sugar cookie

Hey you, Christmas!

Yeah, you in the red and green

Come on over here and give us a hug.

Wow, I'd forgotten that smell of pine.

Where'd you get all those packages?

Well, it's been a year.

And a year is a year if you know what I mean?

But I still love ya. Still love ya.

Now, how's about a kiss—

In keeping with the Season?!

A star shined

Angels sang

Shepherds watched

Wise men trekked

And a Mother loved

Has anyone counted the needles on a Christmas tree
The number of ornaments and lights
The lengths of garland and the heights of stars?

Has anyone measured the size of gift boxes
The yards of ribbon and the feet of paper
The weight of tissue and the "love" on tags?

Has anyone gauged the reasons for giving?

Unless you're a computer

Dates are nothing more than pauses

Ticking away within your heart

Unless you're a computer

Yuletide memories weave together

Creating strings growing richer with time

Unless you're a computer

Smells and colors collide

Continuing the confusion confusing the facts

Unless you're a computer

Lyrical expressions pervade

Enhancing the celebration

Unless you're a computer

As the millennium strikes

Nothing should worry you

Merry Christmas, Happy Millennium

I thought about the first Christmas

And of the angels that hovered over the stable

I thought about their song of peace and good will

And all the people that heeded their call

These past two thousand years

Angels and soldiers hovered above

And around a small village

The streets were crowded

And the crowds were anxious

There was confusion

Lack of water

Lack of room

There was anger

Suspicion

And rocks to be hurled

There was also stillness

And a joyous new birth

To hope, to Christmas,

And a peaceful New Year

The smell of pine greets me through the trickling rain as I pause at a red light. Red with green enhances the tips of the surrounding skyscrapers and the 'Christmas Trees' sign hanging above me.

With the light green I move swiftly swinging my packages down the street. Wreaths and fluttering ribbons soften the brownstones along my path but I have no time to enjoy them as I race to catch a suitcase for a twelve o'clock flight.

At the next corner, shop windows enchant with innocent displays that in another season would not be so enchanting. I am tempted, but the weight of my bargains presses me on towards home.

Another light – an open space – a panoramic view of NYC glistening like a gigantic Christmas present. Even though the light is green I must stop to enjoy the view, to read an imaginary greeting wishing me a safe journey – a good Christmas.

Finally, I reach my door and my doorman's helping hand, which I decline while wishing him an early Merry Christmas. He knows not that I am leaving my city to celebrate in another as bright.

The heart holds Christmas deep within us
Securing our memories, joys and prayers
As it guards family traditions and deeds
It knows the magic of a Christmas Eve
And skips a beat when we're together

Although some angels sometimes look away, their golden auras continue to illuminate.

Although kings, who follow a single star, sometimes question their wisdom, shepherds in a single field don't question theirs when searching for auras among the many stars.

And although a single struggling family dwells at the end of the kings' journey, many families don't; yet angels still sing to them, and people of good will still abide with them under God's many stars.

Merry Christmas

Mama, why is that star shining so brightly?

It is announcing your birth throughout the universe.

The angels, Mama, why do they sing so joyfully?

It is their way of bringing good people to you.

Mama, why are you holding me so closely?

To keep you warm and protect you while I can.

You were born to teach the world,

I was born to teach you love.

Thank you, Mama!

Out of the past and into the future memories explode as tired cardboard boxes pop open and joy creaks out of the creases in the crinkled tissue paper that separates sparkling figurines and stars.

Through tinsel-clad branches and beneath bells and icicle candies wrapped in red cellophane electrical currents spin within braided wires sending fragile flashes of Christmas.

Carols from foreign choirs and songs by bygone singers decode and distort the festive tone faster than the changing of a disc as a simple Silent Night bounces from speaker to wall to ear to heart.

Thirty-three Christmas greetings

Thirty-three celebrations of Christmas

Celebrating the Birth of Christmas –

The birth of a new sense of joy

Of a new song

Sung by angels praying for peace on earth –

Of good will towards mankind

Thirty-three Christmas greetings

Thirty-three expressions of hope

Celebrating the gift of family –

Of friendship

And happiness and love

Thirty-three Christmas greetings

Thirty-three encapsulations of cherished memories!

Celebrating the future we hold

Sail away towards the furthermost star on a northern line as Christmas Eve ebbs – sail away towards the furthermost star at the point of a new Christmas morn where dreams on colossal cumulus clouds dance between double rainbows and glide across celestial transoms, as a fresh winter solstice slightly nudges the tilt on a slumbering orb

Sail away towards the furthermost star with a bygone storyteller at the helm priming hopes and childhood fancies, evoking fables and legends to warm to, as nostalgia navigates through the nebulae so memories can seed at the tip of twilight where all recorded thoughts ignite and wishes are known to take hold at the point of a new Christmas morn.

Merry Christmas!

Stenciled snowflakes across a wide windowpane
Bound triangular trees in green cellophane
Angels with cotton wings and red stars in twos
Sit above inspiring the onlooker's muse

Garlands with bows and bells in clusters of four
Bedeck the whole border completing the tour
Reindeer and sleigh glide up and divert across
On a field of smudged Glasswax adding a gloss

To the right is a moon with a Santa Claus face
With a wreath and a "HO!" for balance and pace
And a Christmas tree's gleam to give it a rush
Stressing the etching's bright Santa-Moon's blush

When snow falls do you think of Christmas – even
if it's early March when you're outside slipping on
some kid's slide, are you humming a leftover
Yuletide tune?

And in mid-July while swinging in a hammock,
swinging way up north under a blanket of stars, and
suddenly snow starts to fall down on your face, do
you run for cover or seek out Santa?

And when in October when a bizarre blizzard hits,
as you slush around in melting grey snow, are reds,
greens and evergreens dancing in your head?

And in late December with fake sparkling
snowdrifts dotting your windows, and spiralling
snow-caps dotting your curb like the topping on a
five-cent Charlotte Russe, do you fancy running
out to play?

Or are you just content staying in, remembering all
those you've shared snow with, and Christmas?

Some sing

Some shop
Some cook
Some clean

Some wrap
Some dress
Some decorate

Some write
Some call
Some pray

Some sing

Generations sit along a long candlelit table feasting on old family recipes, old carols and songs, and tales told at other tables in other homes at other Christmases.

As wine is passed to season a conversation richly celebrating the past, a baby awakes in the next room, and those at the table scurry to make room for a new Christmas memory to begin.

Flexing branches on fake trees

Hanging ornaments, hanging mistletoe

Dragging table leaves from cellars

Carrying folding chairs too

Cleaning everything everywhere

Writing cards, reading cards

Sorting gifts, wrapping gifts

Hiding wrapping paper

Hiding newspapers and bathrobes

Hiding knickknacks under beds

Buying sugar, buying flour

Buying flowers

Baking, cooking and doing more decorating

Making ice

Making room in the refrigerator

Filling the refrigerator

Setting tables

Placing place cards

Unfolding folding chairs

Selecting the music, setting volume, pressing repeat

Lighting trees, dimming lights

Lighting candles

Answering doors

Hugging guests, kissing guests

Exchanging gifts

And wishing the world a Merry Christmas!

Economies

Like Christmas trees

Do come down

But as trends and traditions have shown

They do go back up again

And when they do they look beautiful

And make us all smile

To a Merry Christmas

And a Healthy, Happy

New Year filled with

Pleasurable upticks

The shadow behind the star graciously fades away

As a new dawn –

A new day –

A Christmas Day begins with promise and peace!

It seems snow seems too far away. Yet late summer's sun has ebbed from its overhead noonday perch. The fading tan that fuels your healthy glow is waning, the sand you're shaking from your shoes has lost its magic, and the white back steps you're standing on need sanding

You scan the garden furniture that needs mending, take a deep breath and then another, then look out beyond the weathered red brick patio, beyond the faded beige soil covering the knoll, beyond all those uneven patches of browning crab grass, the hundreds of dangling dandelions you have no time to pluck, beyond the listless leaves that seem hastily pinned to trees.

You keep looking back, way back to the far edge of your opaque garden – back to the point where it bonds so naturally with the natural woodland, and then your eyes take hold of a sturdy young evergreen, shoulder-height and as wide as your extended fingertips, held in a glistening patch of fading sunshine.

And then your heart, your autumn-weary heart, leapfrogs and runs smack into Christmas!

Christmas can be found in enthusiastic wrappings
As well as in the inspired choice of gifts
Not only in the anticipated phone calls
But also in the lasting jovial afterthoughts
Sometimes not just in the clever greeting cards
But in all the familiar signatures

Christmas can be found in the burnt bits
As well as the icing on the cookies
Not only in the bright trimmings and decorations
But also in the magnificent scent of the trees
Sometimes not just in the seasonal melodies
But in joyfully humming along with the carolers

Christmas can be found in the perpetual spirit
As well as in the twelve-day holiday
Not only in the elaborate menus and settings
But also in those sharing the festive table
Sometimes not just in the visit to Santa
But in the person who is standing next to you

In times of stress

When pockets are short

Expenses high and situations uncertain

Just give of your heart

It is the most Christmas of gifts

Could you please be still and listen?

Your boughs are shimmering –

You're so excited I can't get a word in!

Yes, you're bright and sparkly

And so, so ornamented!

Well, I've been collecting for ages

But I suppose you knew that

Do you like your new lights?

"Illuminating" is a choice word

You know you know you look magnificent

Why?

Because I can feel your joy

Speaking of which, how do I look?

We're both happy and merry

All I hope is that I'm as bright

Merry Christmas!

Memories and snowflakes

Magic and illusions

Flavor pots and pans and windowsills

And the icing on Christmas cakes

Standing near a Christmas tree at Christmastime

Making wishes and wishing they be granted

That dreams are realized

Promises kept and love shared

And that the joy known at Christmastime

Will be felt forever

A star – a celestial beacon

Beckoning curious Wise Men

A star – a celestial signpost

Posting the way for timid shepherds

A star – a celestial night-light

Lighting the Child illuminating the world!

Christmas is easy on your heart

Hard on your stomach

Wicked on your wallet

And gentle on your dreams!

There are those angels that while away their time standing atop triumphant arches and flying buttresses trumpeting good news. Others enjoy gathering in enormous numbers on top of enormous celestial clouds and on the heads of pins proclaiming glad tidings.

And then there are those down-to-earth angels down on earth that quietly say, "Supper is ready!", "I'll pick you up!", "I'll watch your cat!", "Let me carry that!", "Here, take my seat!", "Take half of this sandwich!"

These angels always keep in touch, really listen when you ramble, and offer sound advice. And they usually are the first to wish you "A Merry Christmas!" even when it's not their holiday.

POSTSCRIPT

This might sound silly, but my eyes always fill with tears when Santa waves a Merry Christmas hello at the end of the Thanksgiving Day Parade, when the sparkling Rockettes do their tap-tap-tapping and a zillion lights light on The Rockefeller Center tree, and when the ballerinas on toe make the magical Nutcracker Christmas tree grow higher than the Met's proscenium arch.

Tears also come when I bring my fresh evergreen into my home, and again when I plug in the lights accompanied by some nostalgic Bing Crosby holiday tunes. Tears also flow, and I believe will always flow, at the conclusion of such great holiday films as Alastair Sims' "A Christmas Carol," Jimmy Stewart's "It's a Wonderful Life", Bing again with Ingrid Bergman's "The Bells of St. Mary's," Cary Grant and Loretta Young's "The Bishops Wife," and Loretta's "Come to the Stable."

As to TV specials, well, most certainly "The Jackie Gleason Christmas Special," and without a doubt the deeply-felt performance of Geraldine Page in the 1966 TV production of Truman Capote's magnificent "A Christmas Memory." Thank God they're all on video so that the world can enjoy a good cry!

As to families, well, I have a big one and have always enjoyed, more than anything else in the world, our Christmas Eve supper with its twenty-four fish dishes, its countless homemade desserts, hours of holiday music and endless gift-opening parade.

But mostly what elicits tears, which I've learned to hold in through years of practice, is when our toast is made. It has always been short and simple with a "God Bless Us Everyone" tacked on the end. It never mattered who made it or who could hear it over the buzz at our long supper table that sometimes stretched into the next room.

What really mattered was that we raised our glasses in unison, and a toast was made and felt by me and all those I love the most. That feeling, which provokes that hidden tear, must be what Paradise has to be all about.

Lastly, Christmas Eve Midnight Mass: my eyes well up as the clergy and the choir process with the Christ Child and lay Him in the manger to the strains of "Adeste Fideles." This provokes such sweet memories of my childhood, going to school at St. Mary's Star of the Sea, and all the religious stories I have ever heard.

Then later at mass when the Gospel is read, starting with "And it came to pass…" I sit back as if I was being tucked into bed and someone is reading "Once upon a time…" to me. At that apex Heaven and Earth and all that dwell in and between, including both the angels and saints, rock me in an awakened sleep like none other, and as the Gospel

ends with its "Good will towards men!" a joyful
tear falls because I'm so happy.

And yes one last tear – when my January American
Express bill arrives!

Glorious is Christmas!
Glorious when you believe in it
Glorious when you love it
Glorious – what else?!

Other holiday works by Vito Gentile:

Little Christmas, a delightful romp looking back from a park bench in London to a nineteen-fifties Brooklyn.

Guests at the Stable, a children's Nativity play with book and lyrics by Gentile and music by Bradley Hull.

Things to do on Christmas Eve, a collection of nine short insightful plays with characters whose paths cross during a long and hurried Christmas Eve.

For information regarding purchasing a book or scheduling a production, please contact August First Arts at P.O. Box 311, East Quogue, NY 11942, or at augustfirstarts@aol.com.